Word Puzzles

This book belongs to

_____

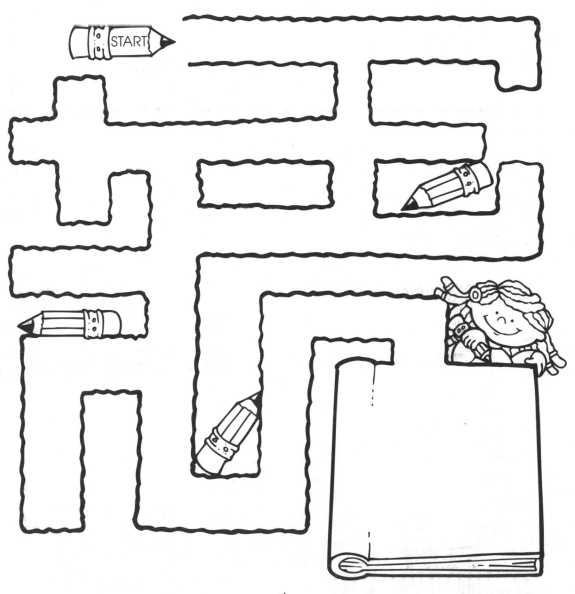

START

Name _____

Mixed-Up Bs

Unscramble the words that name the pictures.
Write the words.

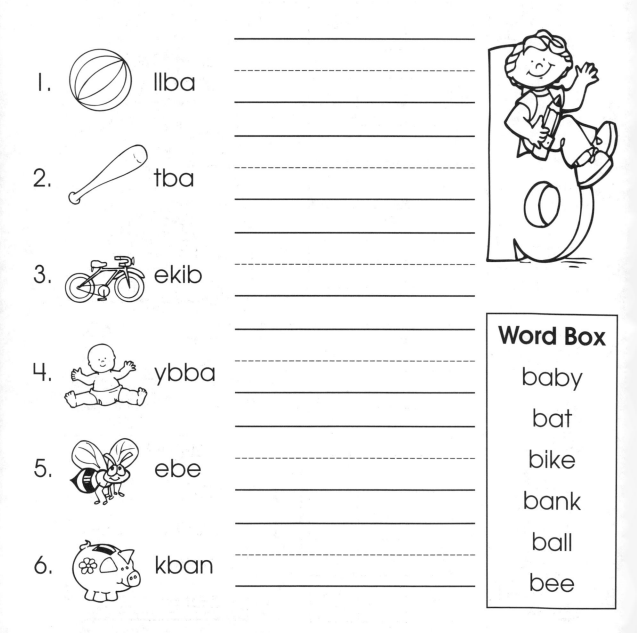

1. llba _____

2. tba _____

3. ekib _____

4. ybba _____

5. ebe _____

6. kban _____

Word Box

baby

bat

bike

bank

ball

bee

FS109024 Word Puzzles

Name _____

See What You Can C

Use the words in the Word Box to help you write the names of the pictures.

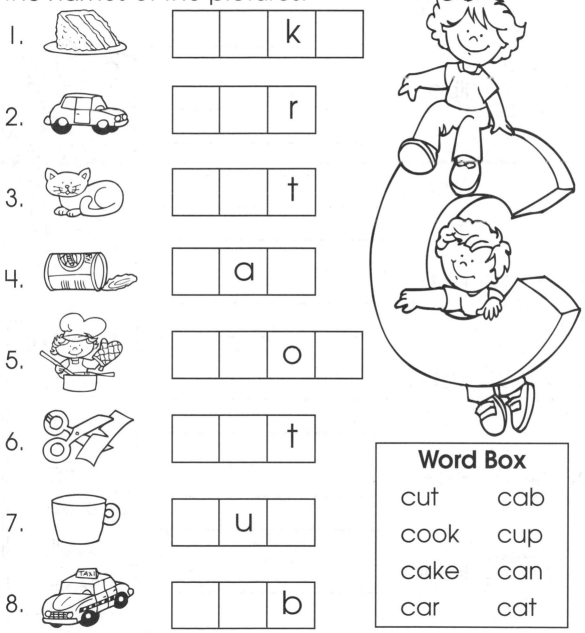

1. | | | k | |

2. | | | r |

3. | | | t |

4. | | a | |

5. | | | o | |

6. | | | t |

7. | | u | |

8. | | | b |

Word Box

cut	cab
cook	cup
cake	can
car	cat

3
reproducible

Name _____

Three in a Row

Color the pictures whose words rhyme with **can**.

fan	man	pan
cat	ran	ten
pig	bed	van

4
reproducible

FS109024 Word Puzzles

Name _____

Fill Them In

Write the vowels to complete each word.

Floating High

Color the words that start with **e** orange.
Color the words that start with **f** yellow.
Write the words under the correct beginning
letters below.

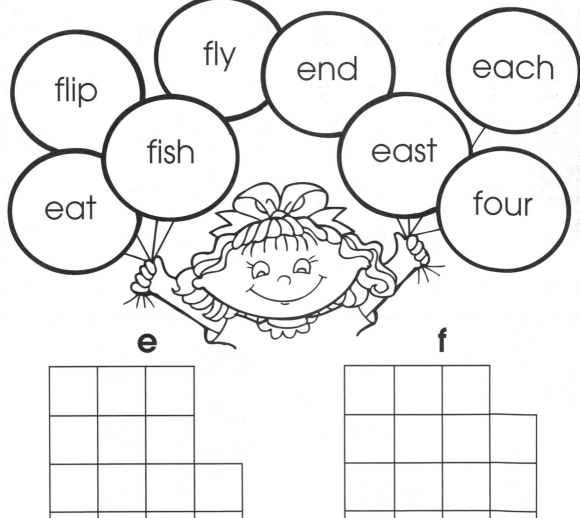

e

f

Name _____

Time for G, H, and I

Find and circle the words in the puzzle.
The words go → and ↓.

d	g	i	f	t	w	j	t	e	g
h	i	g	m	n	h	a	n	b	i
a	r	l	h	e	a	r	t	q	r
n	s	o	e	l	t	d	o	y	a
d	m	o	v	x	m	h	u	r	f
i	c	e	c	r	e	a	m	l	f
z	g	i	r	l	r	f	p	c	e

giraffe   igloo

ice cream   girl

heart   hat

hand   gift

Name _____

Let's Play

Use the words in the Word Box to help you write the name of each picture.

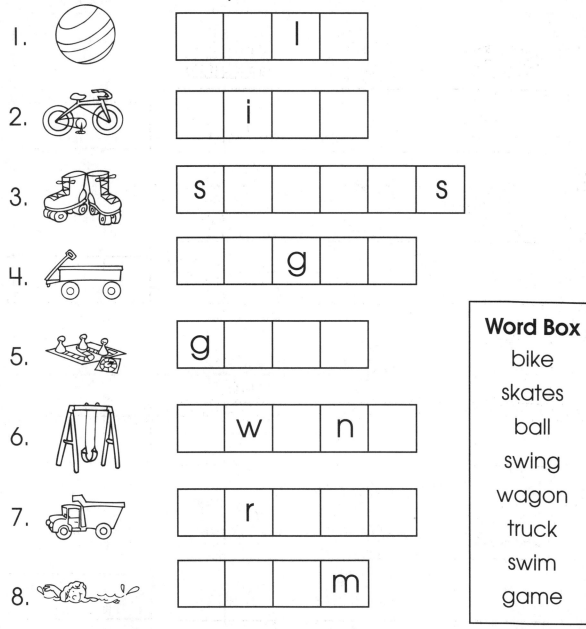

1. | | | l | |

2. | | i | | |

3. | s | | | | | s |

4. | | | g | | |

5. | g | | | |

6. | | w | | n | |

7. | | r | | | |

8. | | | | m |

Word Box
bike
skates
ball
swing
wagon
truck
swim
game

FS109024 Word Puzzles

New Word Fun

Write the first letter for each picture.
Write the letters in the boxes to make a new word.

1.

2.

3.

4.

Scrambled Js, Ks, and Ls

Unscramble the words that name the pictures.
Write the words.

1.  nkitet _____

2.  kngi _____

3.  mlap _____

4.  elg _____

5.  kiet _____

6.  scajk _____

Word Box

kite

king

leg

jacks

kitten

lamp

Name _____

Fruity Fun

Read the word for each picture.
Write the words in the puzzle.

Across

2. plum
3. apple
5. grapes

Down

1. orange
2. pear
4. peach

FS109024 Word Puzzles

Crack the Code

Write the missing letters for each word.
Use the code at the bottom of the page.

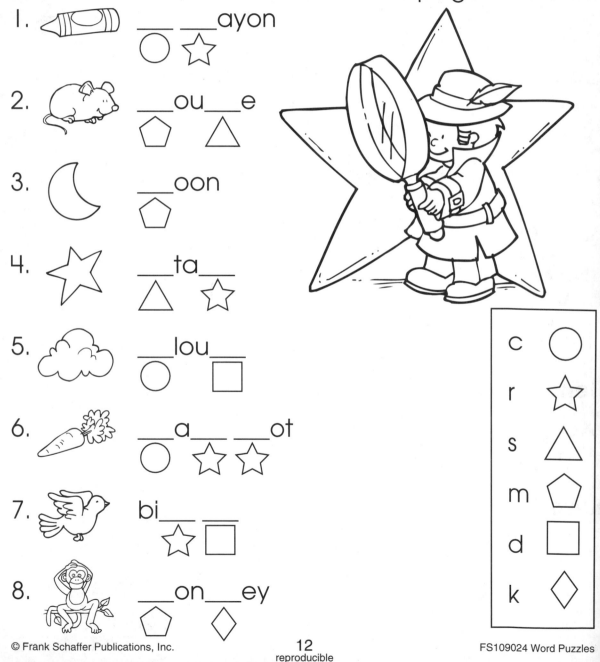

1. ___ ___ayon
   ○ ☆

2. ___ou___e
   ⬠ △

3. ___oon
   ⬠

4. ___ta___
   △ ☆

5. ___lou___
   ○ ☐

6. ___a___ ___ot
   ○ ☆ ☆

7. bi___ ___
   ☆ ☐

8. ___on___ey
   ⬠ ◇

c	○
r	☆
s	△
m	⬠
d	☐
k	◇

FS109024 Word Puzzles

Name _____

Number Connector

Connect the number words in order.
Then color the number you made.

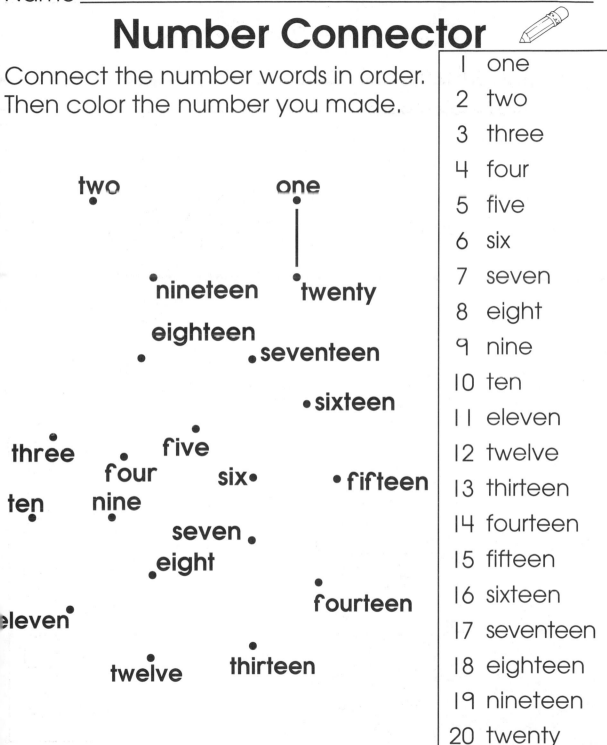

1	one
2	two
3	three
4	four
5	five
6	six
7	seven
8	eight
9	nine
10	ten
11	eleven
12	twelve
13	thirteen
14	fourteen
15	fifteen
16	sixteen
17	seventeen
18	eighteen
19	nineteen
20	twenty

two   one

nineteen   twenty

eighteen
seventeen

sixteen

three   five
four   six   fifteen
ten   nine
seven
eight
fourteen
eleven
twelve   thirteen

Counting Critters

Count the things in each group. Write the number word in the boxes by the pictures.

1 one	2 two	3 three	4 four
5 five	6 six	7 seven	8 eight
9 nine	10 ten	11 eleven	12 twelve

1.

2.

3.

4.

5.

6.

14
reproducible

Fun Foods

Write each word in the correct place.
Color the pictures.

| popcorn | ice cream | lollipop |
| candy | cookie | cake |

1.

2.

3.

4.

5.

6.

Name _____

In My Garden

Find and circle the words in the puzzle.
The words go → and ↓.

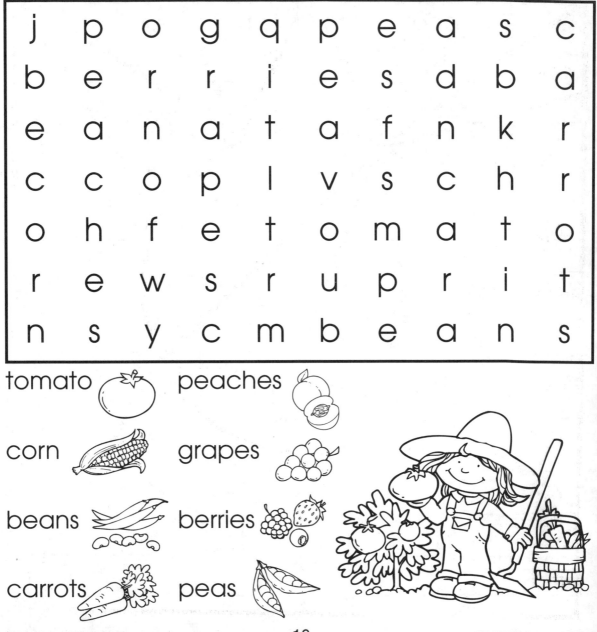

j	p	o	g	q	p	e	a	s	c
b	e	r	r	i	e	s	d	b	a
e	a	n	a	t	a	f	n	k	r
c	c	o	p	l	v	s	c	h	r
o	h	f	e	t	o	m	a	t	o
r	e	w	s	r	u	p	r	i	t
n	s	y	c	m	b	e	a	n	s

tomato   peaches

corn   grapes

beans   berries

carrots   peas

16
reproducible

FS109024 Word Puzzles

Name _____

Awesome Animals

Find and circle the words in the puzzle.
The words go → and ↓.

elephant   horse

giraffe   whale

alligator   snake

dolphin   zebra

turtle   monkey

q	h	w	b	j	t	u	r	t	l	e
m	o	n	k	e	y	k	g	p	c	l
i	r	s	p	g	i	r	a	f	f	e
g	s	l	d	o	f	w	o	n	l	p
z	e	b	r	a	f	h	e	r	h	h
d	a	l	l	i	g	a	t	o	r	a
m	f	r	u	d	o	l	p	h	i	n
s	n	a	k	e	r	e	v	a	k	t

Get a Clue!

Name _____

Write the word that rhymes with the bold word in each sentence.

1. Tommy likes to **play** all ⬚⬚⬚ .

2. The fish got my **net** ⬚⬚ .

3. The color of her **bed** is ⬚⬚ .

4. Kara has **fun** in the ⬚⬚⬚ .

5. The **boy** had a ⬚⬚ .

6. Lindsay lost her **small** blue ⬚⬚⬚ .

7. Dad's **tie** fell in his ⬚⬚ .

8. She served the **fish** on the ⬚⬚⬚ .

wet
ball
sun
dish
toy
day
red
pie

FS109024 Word Puzzles

Name _____

School Tools

Find and circle the words in the puzzle.
The words go → and ↓.

pencil	paper	eraser	chalk	scissors
crayons	marker	book	glue	ruler

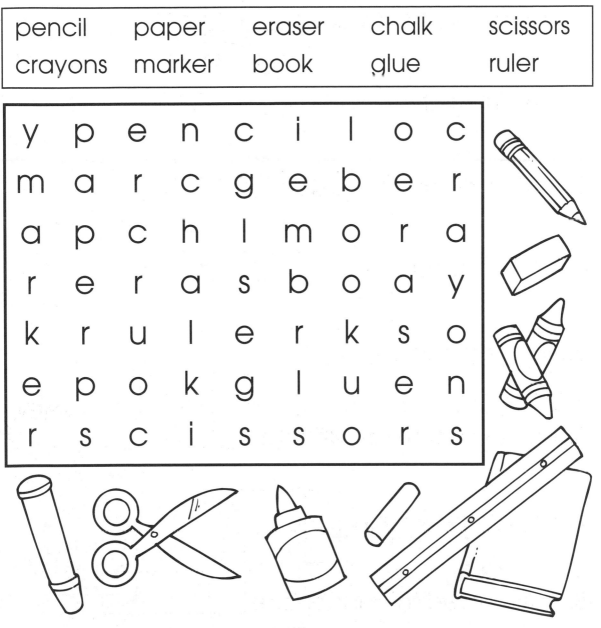

```
y  p  e  n  c  i  l  o  c
m  a  r  c  g  e  b  e  r
a  p  c  h  l  m  o  r  a
r  e  r  a  s  b  o  a  y
k  r  u  l  e  r  k  s  o
e  p  o  k  g  l  u  e  n
r  s  c  i  s  s  o  r  s
```

FS109024 Word Puzzles

Name _____

Make Your Own Words

Write the first letter for each picture. Write the letters in the boxes to make a new word.

1.

2.

3.

4.

Name _____

Look and Color

Color the following words red.

the	was	on	and	but

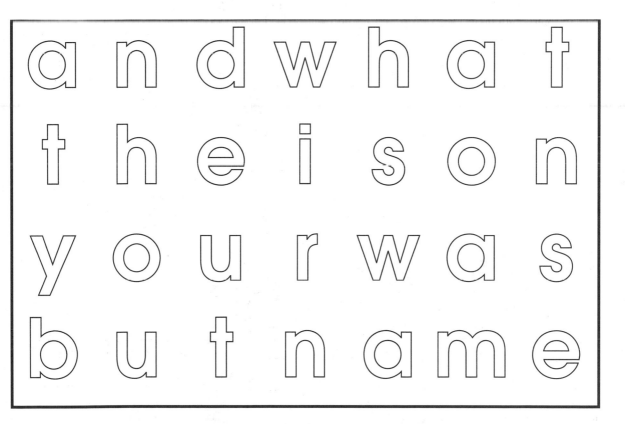

a n d w h a t
t h e i s o n
y o u r w a s
b u t n a m e

Write the words you did not color to make
a sentence.

_____

- ?

_____

FS109024 Word Puzzles

A Lost Ball

Help Tommy find his ball.
Follow the words in ABC order.

dog

hair

egg

ape

bunny

cat

gift

cab

donkey

apple

fish

eating

nest

gate

flower

FS109024 Word Puzzles

Name _____

Megan's Birthday Present

Write a word from the Word Box to complete each sentence.

1. Megan got a new __ __ __ __.

2. It was a birthday __ __ __ __.

3. The color is __ __ __ __ __.

4. Megan wears a __ __ __ __ __ __ when she rides a bike.

5. She wears elbow __ __ __ __.

6. She wears __ __ __ __ pads, too.

Word Box

green   bike   pads

helmet   knee   gift

FS109024 Word Puzzles

Name _____

Wanting a Web

Help the spider get to its web.
Follow the words in ABC order.

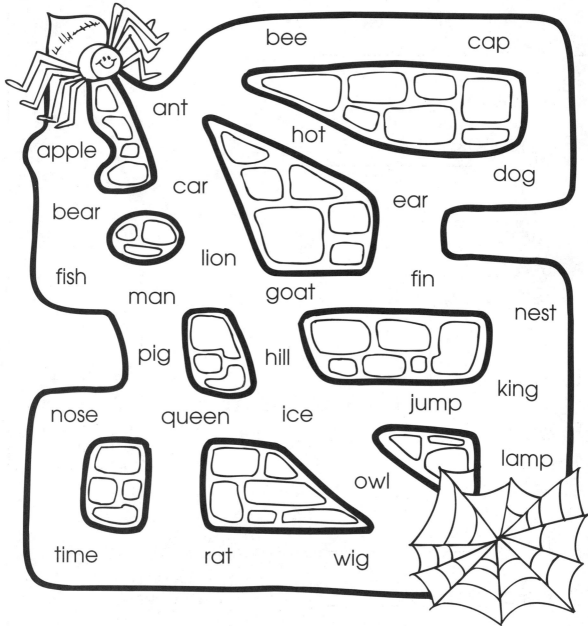

bee

cap

ant

hot

apple

dog

car

ear

bear

lion

fish

fin

man

goat

nest

pig

hill

king

nose

queen

ice

jump

lamp

owl

time

rat

wig

24
reproducible

Name _____

Lining Them Up

Unscramble and write the number words.

1. nnei ___ ___ ___ ___

2. neves ___ ___ ___ ___ ___

3. wetlev ___ ___ ___ ___ ___ ___

4. etreh ___ ___ ___ ___ ___

5. xis ___ ___ ___

6. etn ___ ___ ___

7. neo ___ ___ ___

8. efvi ___ ___ ___ ___

9. eeenlv ___ ___ ___ ___ ___ ___

10. wot ___ ___ ___

11. theig ___ ___ ___ ___ ___

12. rufo ___ ___ ___ ___

| one |
| two |
| three |
| four |
| five |
| six |
| seven |
| eight |
| nine |
| ten |
| eleven |
| twelve |

Time to Rhyme

Use the picture clues to match the rhyming words.

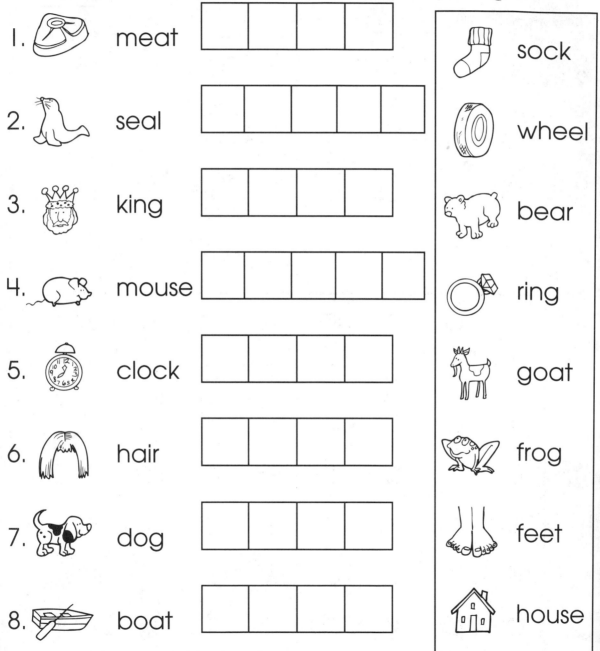

1. meat

2. seal

3. king

4. mouse

5. clock

6. hair

7. dog

8. boat

sock

wheel

bear

ring

goat

frog

feet

house

FS109024 Word Puzzles

Name _____

Search and Circle

Fill in the blanks with **dr**, **fr**, **gr**, or **tr**. Find and circle the words in the puzzle.

1. _____ame

2. _____ain

3. _____uck

4. _____eam

5. _____ee

6. _____ive

7. _____uit

8. _____ass

b	g	r	a	i	v	e	w
f	r	u	i	t	g	r	a
x	a	f	e	r	r	n	f
u	i	d	r	e	a	m	r
i	n	r	x	e	s	r	a
t	r	u	c	k	s	l	m
o	p	k	d	r	i	v	e

FS109024 Word Puzzles

Name _____

Splishing and Splashing

Color the spaces with rhyming words **gray**.
Color the other spaces **blue**.

_an

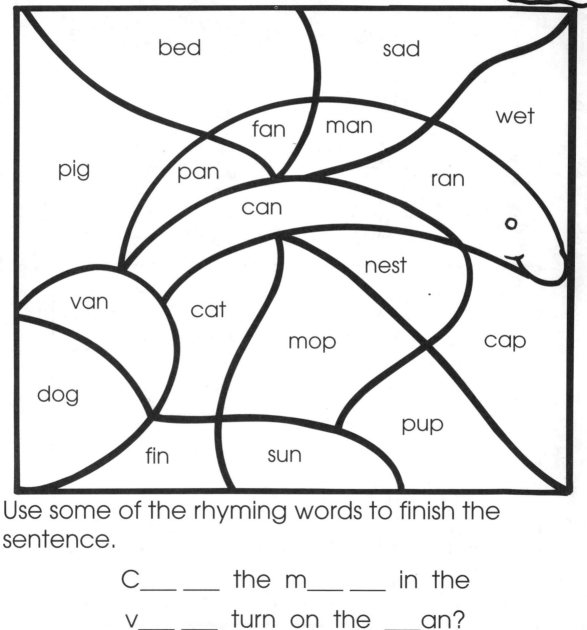

Use some of the rhyming words to finish the
sentence.

C___ ___ the m___ ___ in the

v___ ___ turn on the ___an?

FS109024 Word Puzzles

Name _____

Boxy Fun

Write the missing letters in the puzzle.
Use the words in the Word Box.

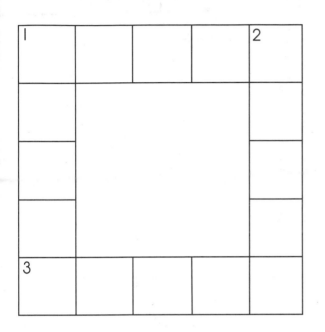

Across

1.

3.

Down

1.

2.

Word Box

paint

toast

peach

heart

29
reproducible

FS109024 Word Puzzles

Q + U

Use the pictures to help you read the words.
Write the words in the puzzle.

Across

1.  quiet

3. quarter

4. quail

5. unicorn

Down

2. umbrella

4. queen

Name _____

Fix These Words

Unscramble the letters. Use the pictures to help you. Write the words on the lines.

| g | p | i |

| r | a | t | s |

| u | n | s |

| d | e | b |

| t | h | a |

| n | f | a |

| t | e | n | s |

| u | b | s |

Name _____

Find the Rhymes

Write the rhyming words in the puzzle boxes.
Then write the words in the silly sentence below.

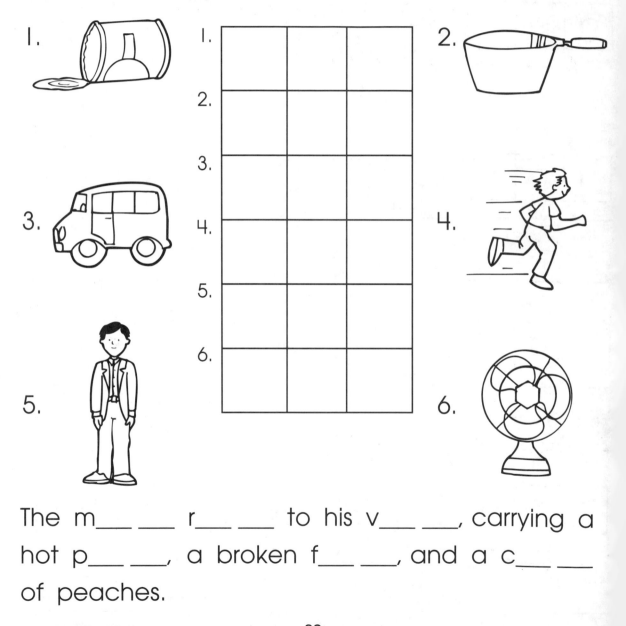

The m__ __ r__ __ to his v__ __, carrying a

hot p__ __, a broken f__ __, and a c__ __

of peaches.

Name _____

Nifty New Words

Write the first letter for each picture.
Read the new word. Draw a picture of it in the box.

1.

2.

3.

FS109024 Word Puzzles

Name _____

Hungry Birds

Help the birds find the worms.
Color the boxes in ABC order.

		ape	hug	fox
		ball	star	gas
deer	cake	cut	door	leg
fan	lake	man	ear	fish
kite	jet	ice	land	goat
lips	king	joke	igloo	hat
map	bed	rose	net	kiss
nose	owl	pet	quit	

FS109024 Word Puzzles

Puzzling Words

Fill in the blanks with **s, sl, sm, sn,** or **st**.
Write the words in the puzzle.

1. 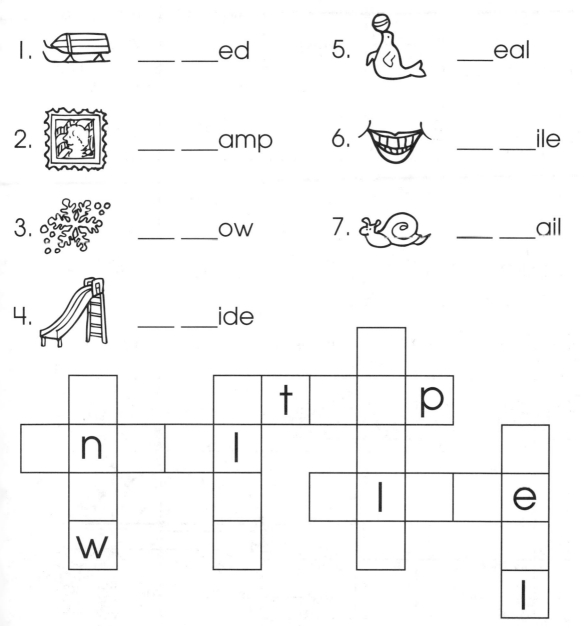 ___ ___ed

5. ___eal

2. ___ ___amp

6. ___ ___ile

3. ___ ___ow

7. ___ ___ail

4. ___ ___ide

FS109024 Word Puzzles

Name _____

Shapely Words

Use a word from the Word Box to finish each sentence. Then use the words in the puzzle.

Across ———————————

1. The _____ crept across the grass.

3. I pulled Kevin in the _____ .

Down ———————————

1. I like to play in _____ .

2. The _____ roared.

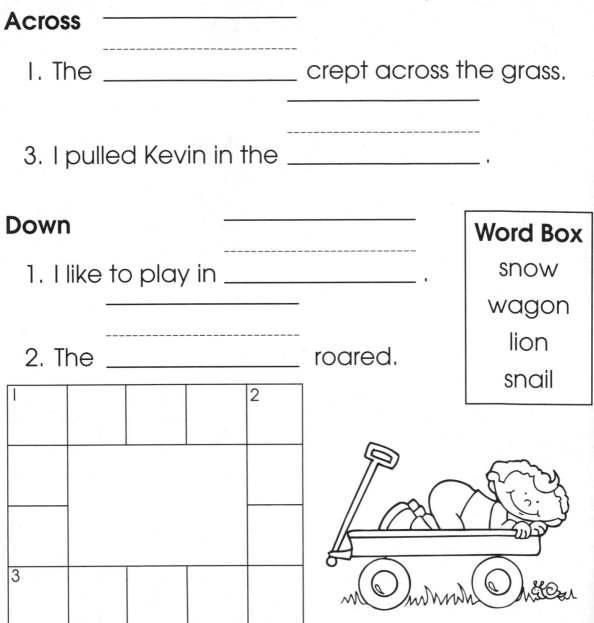

Name _____

New Word Fun

Read about Ty's day. Write the times in the puzzle.

1. Ty wakes up at 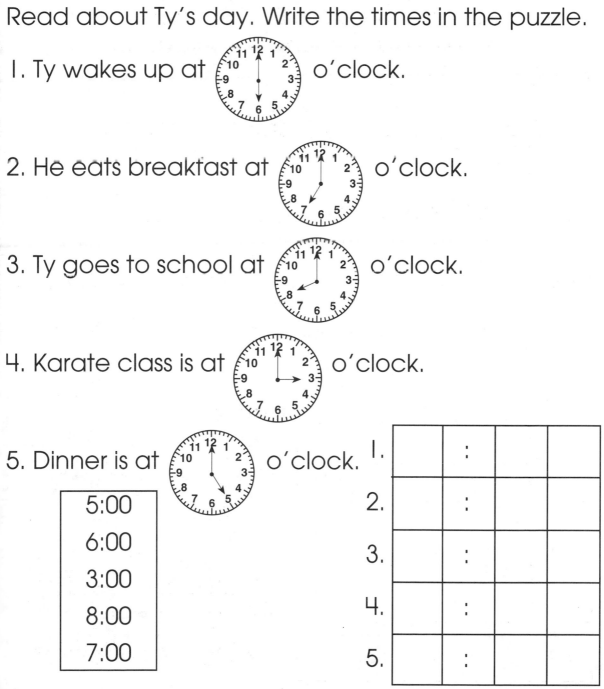 o'clock.

2. He eats breakfast at o'clock.

3. Ty goes to school at o'clock.

4. Karate class is at o'clock.

5. Dinner is at o'clock.

| 5:00 |
| 6:00 |
| 3:00 |
| 8:00 |
| 7:00 |

1.

2.

3.

4.

5.

FS109024 Word Puzzles

Living or Not?

Color the pictures of living things.

pony	pig	ball
doll	lamb	snowman
rain	chicken	duck

Name _____

Let's Go!

Color the spaces with words for ways to travel.

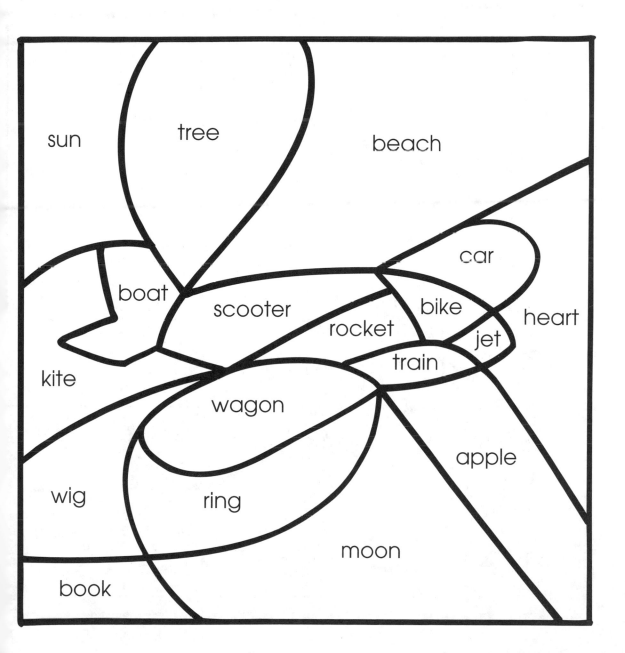

sun

tree

beach

boat

scooter

car

bike

rocket

jet

heart

kite

train

wagon

apple

wig

ring

moon

book

Name _____

What a Great Day!

Read the color words. Color the spaces to match.

40
reproducible

FS109024 Word Puzzles

Name _____

Hot and Sunny

Color the spaces with long vowel words **yellow**.
Color the spaces with short vowel words **blue**.

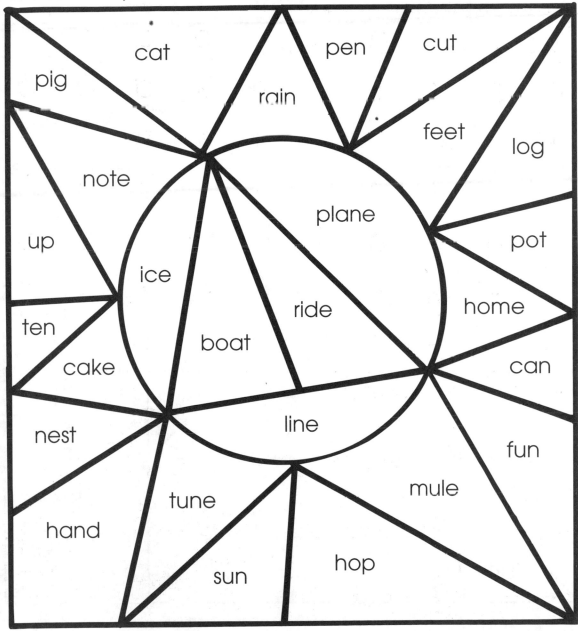

FS109024 Word Puzzles

Name _____

Perfect Patterns

Color the spaces with short vowel words **green**.
Color the spaces with long vowel words **orange**.

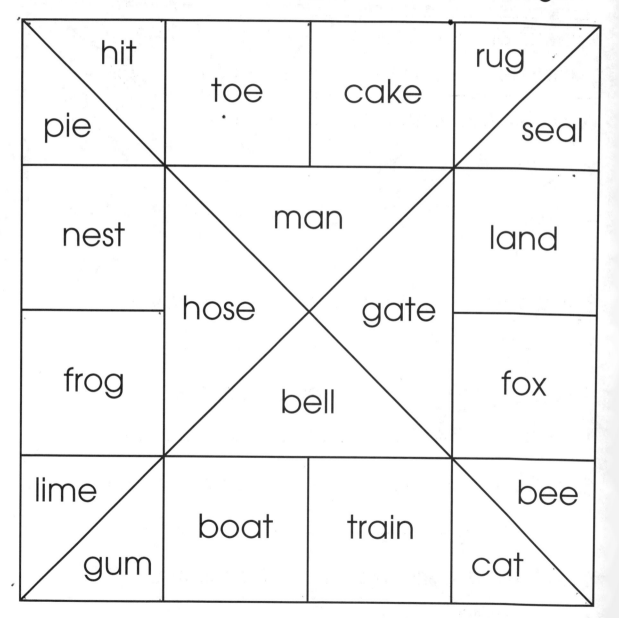

Name _____

Figure Them Out

Unscramble each word. Be sure that it matches the meaning.

teacher	ice cream	apple
mouse	jogger	tennis

1. Someone who runs is called a

   rjggeo __ __ __ __ __ __.

2. A game that uses a racket and a small ball is

   stinne __ __ __ __ __ __.

3. Something cold to eat on a hot day is

   cie ramec __ __ __ __ __ __ __ __.

4. Someone who teaches children is a

   erhteac __ __ __ __ __ __ __ .

5. A tasty fruit that grows on a tree is called an

   leppa __ __ __ __ __ .

6. A furry little animal that squeaks is a

   somue __ __ __ __ __.

Name _____

Double Trouble

Write each word in the box next to a word in the puzzle to make a new word.

bell	walk	ground	room
box	ball	fish	print

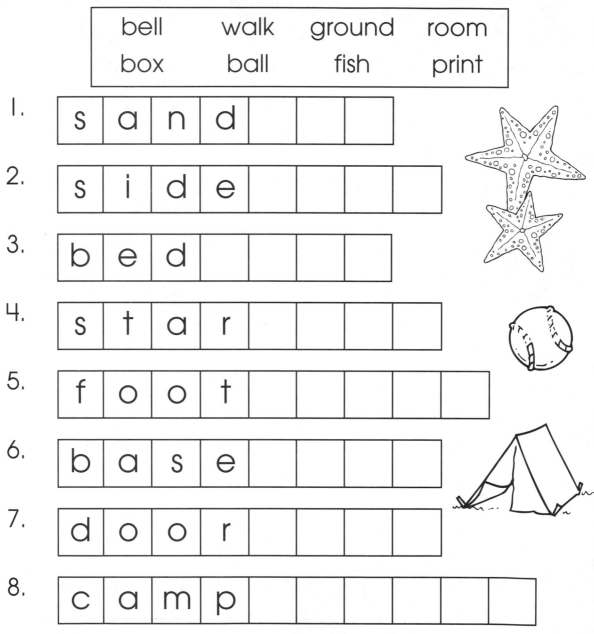

1. | s | a | n | d | | | |

2. | s | i | d | e | | | | |

3. | b | e | d | | | | |

4. | s | t | a | r | | | | |

5. | f | o | o | t | | | | | |

6. | b | a | s | e | | | | |

7. | d | o | o | r | | | | |

8. | c | a | m | p | | | | | |

FS109024 Word Puzzles

Sweet Babies

Write the names of the baby animals in the puzzle.
Use the words in the box to help you.

fawn

calf

duckling

puppy

kitten

A Colorful Creation

Read the words.
Color each box the
color of the thing
named in the box.

banana	grass	pumpkin
carrot	strawberry	sky
water	sun	grasshopper

Name _____

A Secret Sentence

Color the following words in the puzzle **green**.

camp	when	test	time

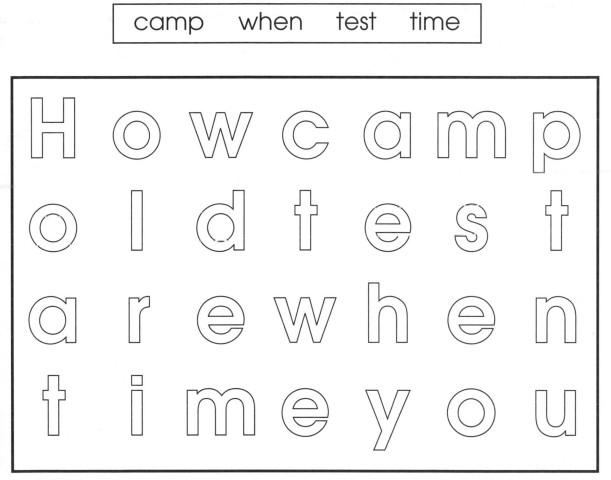

```
H o w c a m p
o l d t e s t
a r e w h e n
t i m e y o u
```

Write the words you did not color to make a sentence.

_____ ?

FS109024 Word Puzzles

Name _____

What a Great Place!

Fill in the puzzle with words that name the pictures below. Use the Word Box to help you.

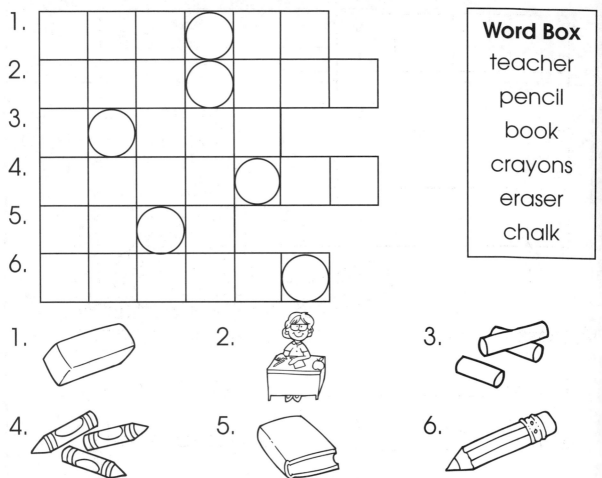

Word Box
teacher
pencil
book
crayons
eraser
chalk

The letters in the circles going down spell a mystery word. The word names a place where all these things can be found.

Write the word. _____

FS109024 Word Puzzles

Name _____

Squaring Up

Use a word from the box to complete each sentence. Then write each word in the puzzle.

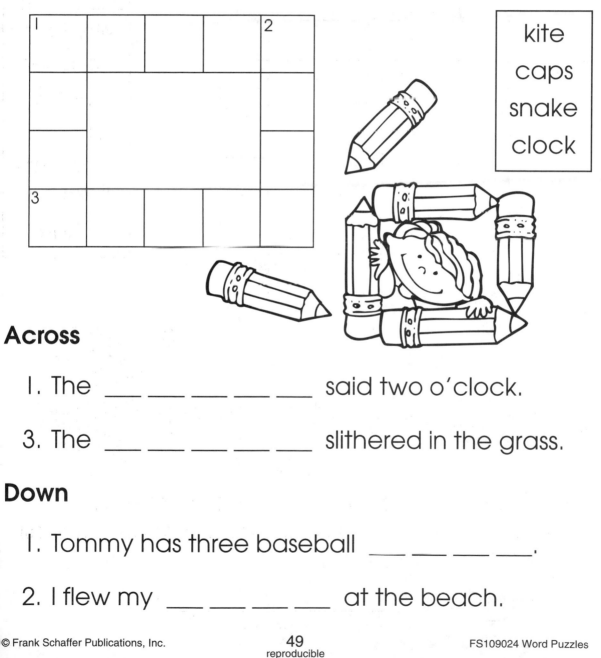

kite

caps

snake

clock

Across

1. The ___ ___ ___ ___ ___ said two o'clock.

3. The ___ ___ ___ ___ ___ slithered in the grass.

Down

1. Tommy has three baseball ___ ___ ___ ___.

2. I flew my ___ ___ ___ ___ at the beach.

FS109024 Word Puzzles

Fun Foods

Write the food words in the puzzle.
Use the Word Box to check your spelling.

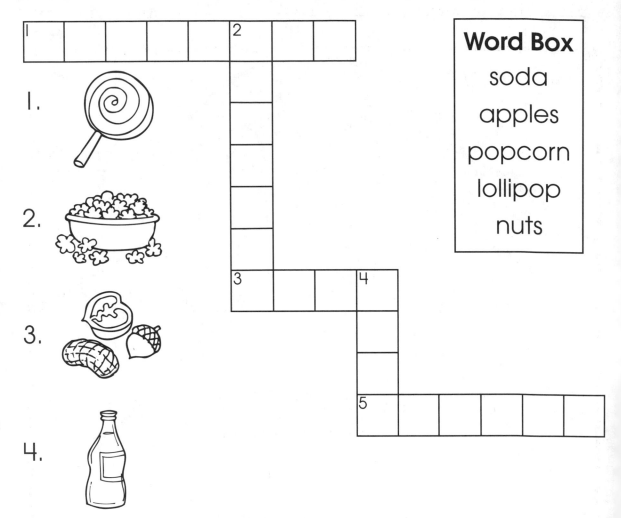

Word Box

soda

apples

popcorn

lollipop

nuts

1.

2.

3.

4.

5.

FS109024 Word Puzzles

Name _____

Up, Up, and Away

Color the spaces with things that we eat **blue**.
Color the spaces with things that we wear **yellow**.
Color the spaces with things that we ride in **green**.

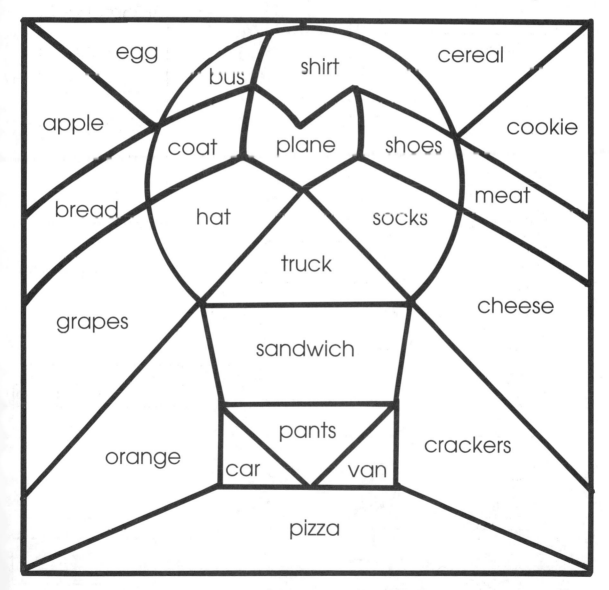

Figure It Out

Write the first letter for each picture. Write the
letters in the boxes to make a new word.

1.

2.

3.

4.

Answer Key

Page 2
1. ball   2. bat
3. bike   4. baby
5. bee   6. bank

Page 3
1. cake 2. car 3. cat
4. can 5. cook 6. cut
7. cup 8. cab

Page 4

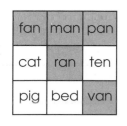

fan	man	pan
cat	ran	ten
pig	bed	van

Page 5

Page 6
Word order may vary.
e: end, eat, each, east
f: fly, fish, four, flip

Page 7

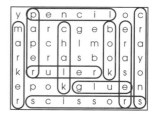

Page 8
1. ball   2. bike
3. skates   4. wagon
5. game   6. swing
7. truck   8. swim

Page 9
1. pig   2. fan
3. bug   4. mop

Page 10
1. kitten   2. king
3. lamp   4. leg
5. kite   6. jacks

Page 11

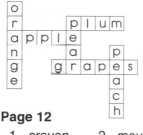

Page 12
1. crayon   2. mouse
3. moon   4. star
5. cloud   6. carrot
7. bird   8. monkey

Page 13

Page 14
1. seven   2. eleven
3. nine   4. three
5. eight   6. five

Page 15
1. popcorn   2. ice cream
3. candy   4. cake
5. cookie   6. lollipop

Page 16

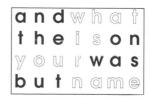

Page 17

Page 18
1. day 2. wet 3. red
4. sun 5. toy 6. ball
7. pie 8. dish

Page 19

Page 20
1. mug 2. ice
3. cat 4. egg

Page 21

and what
the is on
your **was**
but name

What is your name?

Answer Key

Page 22

Page 23

1. bike   2. gift
3. green   4. helmet
5. pads   6. knee

Page 24

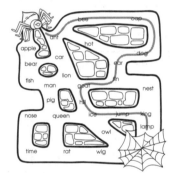

Page 25

1. nine   2. seven
3. twelve   4. three
5. six   6. ten
7. one   8. five
9. eleven   10. two
11. eight   12. four

Page 26

1. feet   2. wheel
3. ring   4. house
5. sock   6. bear
7. frog   8. goat

Page 27

1. frame   2. grain
3. truck   4. dream
5. tree   6. drive
7. fruit   8. grass

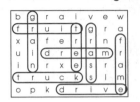

Page 28

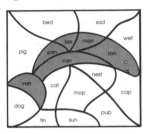

Can the man in the van turn on the fan?

Page 29

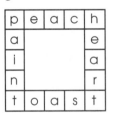

Page 30

Page 31

pig,   star;
sun,   bed;
hat,   fan;
nest,   bus

Page 32

1. can   2. pan
3. van   4. ran
5. man   6. fan

The man ran to his van, carrying a hot pan, a broken fan, and a can of peaches.

Page 33

Check drawings.
1. map   2. net
3. cat

Page 34

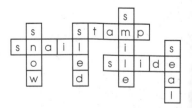

Page 35

1. sled   2. stamp
3. snow   4. slide
5. seal   6. smile
7. snail

Answer Key

Page 36

s	n	a	i	l
n				i
o				o
w	a	g	o	n

Page 37

1. 6:00   2. 7:00   3. 8:00
4. 3:00   5. 5:00

Page 38

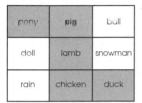

pony	pig	ball
doll	lamb	snowman
rain	chicken	duck

Page 39

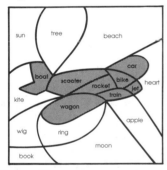

Page 40

The child should color the page according to the directions.

Page 41

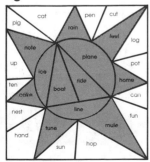

Page 42

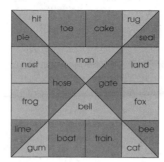

Page 43

1. jogger   2. tennis
3. ice cream 4. teacher
5. apple   6. mouse

Page 44

1. sandbox   2. sidewalk
3. bedroom   4. starfish
5. footprint 6. baseball
7. doorbell
8. campground

Page 45

Page 46

banana (yellow)	grass (green)	pumpkin (orange)
carrot (orange)	strawberry (red)	sky (blue)
water (blue)	sun (yellow)	grasshopper (green)

Page 47

How old are you?

Page 48

1. eraser   2. teacher
3. chalk   4. crayons
5. book   6. pencil

school

Page 49

c	l	o	c	k
a				i
p				t
s	n	a	k	e

Page 50

l	o	l	l	i	p	o	p
					o		
					p		
					c		
					o		
					r		
			n	u	t	s	
						o	
						d	
					a	p	p	l	e	s

Page 51

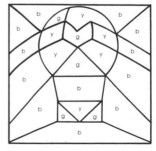

Page 52

1. bed   2. man
3. fun   4. top

FS109024 Word Puzzles

_____ **is**

perfectly wonderful
at working
word puzzles!

Way to go!

_____
signature

_____
date

FS109024 Word Puzzles